T0367954

LETTERS
FROM JESUS

LETTERS FROM JESUS

Poems of Guidance

REGINA MARIE BLAYLOCK

Archway Publishing books may be ordered through booksellers or by contacting:

Archway Publishing
1663 Liberty Drive
Bloomington, IN 47403
www.archwaypublishing.com
844-669-3957

Artist: Regina Marie Blaylock (A.K.A Gina)
Photographer: Kaylee Blaylock

ISBN: 978-1-6657-6123-9 (sc)
ISBN: 978-1-6657-6125-3 (hc)
ISBN: 978-1-6657-6124-6 (e)

Library of Congress Control Number: 2024911552

Print information available on the last page.

Archway Publishing rev. date: 07/30/2024

DEDICATION

"Sometimes I wonder,
How I will ever
Overcome my adversaries.
Then God, moves a mountain
And shines a light
On my spirit,
So, I can journey on."
Gina

I dedicate this book to Jesus because he said, "Knock and the door shall be opened", "Seek and ye shall find". I cried out in the night. I needed help. I was lost and weary. I was numb and knew I had to rise up against, a strong person. He came and wiped off my tears. He brought me along a journey of hope and salvation. He keeps righting the wrongs, even those that are inflicted upon me by the judgements and false perceptions of others. Jesus was there and he has never left my side. He protected me. I know that I am loved. Jesus is my, Savior and he will never let go!

INTRODUCTION

This book is about how God guided me through much pain and suffering during a time when everyone around me chastised and shunned me. I was away from my children and my family believed the lies and gossip of others. No one was on my side but God. God gave me the pen and a voice. He wanted to help me through the confusion. He wanted me to ask questions so he could show me the truths. He wanted me to let go of the pain and understand his purpose for my life. I was always coming to the rescue when someone needed help but when I needed help no one believed me. God was right beside me showing me the way. He kept me quiet and put the pen in my hand. Every day he told me I was beautiful and worthy. He told me the confusion and pain would dissipate. He would bring me to peace and calm.

God taught me to let go. He picked up the baggage and carried it. Now, I look around me, at all my poetry on tiles and think that is the weight I have been carrying around. There are things in life. Trials we must go through so that he can rise us up higher than before. He wants our paths to be ones that point to him. Every time, I stumble he is there to pick me up. His love is beautiful, and he never let's go.

God explained to me that everyone thinks they are right. In the moment they stand up and throw stones that inflict hurt on others. But God is there to protect us from the pain. God helped me to examine my heart and to walk closer to him. He taught me to stand strong and to walk in peace. I do stand up for what I believe in, and he is there keeping me safe. He has parted the water and turned frozen hearts around. In this journey he has taught me his purpose is not all about me. But, through me he can change the world around me. God picks each of us for a purpose in this life that benefits all of us. As we draw closer to him, he shapes us for this purpose. He has walked me around in the silence and shown me the changes he has made through adversity when I walk closer to him. The world around me is changing and so many people have been helped and deterioration has been restored anew.

God is love. His love endures forever. In this book I reveal the poems I sent to my True Love in the midst, of the confusion and devastation. God took ahold of me and revealed to me that he has loved me for a long time, long before I knew it. He revealed that this was, "A Love Story". I am overwhelmed by God's enduring love for me. I am blessed. I hope that this book touches others to know my story wasn't all rainbows and roses. There were many thorns on my path. But God never stops loving us and taking care of us. He is our gift. He has given us Jesus to help intercede and guide us on this journey of life.

CONTENTS

CHAPTER ONE

Walking Out of the Storm

As I am on this journey with God, I have witnessed many miracles in my life. He is shaping me and making me stronger. I have witnessed the fall of giants and mountains moved so I may follow the path he has laid out for me. These collections of poems and letters are how God guided me through the fire and brimstone. I have witnessed his almighty strength and his overwhelming love and protection. He has shown me how he can keep opening the road that I see is blocked. He tells me to keep persevering and he will move every mountain in the way. I am overwhelmed by his deep compassion and love for me. I have learned I am nothing in my own strength but with the strength of God I can do anything if I just believe and trust in him. I hope you enjoy this collection, and it moves you to find a deeper meaning in life with God.

*Psalms 49: 1-7 "Hear this, all ye people; give
ear, all ye inhabitants of the world:
Both low and high, rich and poor, together.
My mouth shall speak of wisdom; and the meditation
of my heart shall be of understanding.
I will incline mine ear to a parable: I will
open my dark saying upon the harp.
Wherefore should I fear in the days of evil, when the
iniquity of my heels shall compass me about?
They that trust in their wealth, and boast themselves
in the multitude of their riches;
None of them can by any means redeem his brother,
nor give to God a ransom for him:" (KJV)*

THEY THOUGHT I WAS HAPPY

I was always happy
They thought
I was always content
Never complaining
I was always courteous
Trying to do what is right
I kept thinking
I didn't measure up
I was easy to get along with
I tried to please
But they always teased
I was kind and caring
Serving God by helping others
I trusted everyone
And tried to give them
My respect
I leant a helping hand
To those who cried out
But they did not know
What I had to bear
I did not know
Why these difficulties
Were burdened me
I had no power in my home
I learned to cope
Keep silent
Don't create waves
Don't ask for the things
I like or want
Take what is given
Remain silent
Clean up the messes

Be chastised and scorned
For wanting a better life
Trying to make a nice life
For my children
Where they are protected,
Nurtured and guided
They didn't see all the
Fires I kept putting out
Tirelessly
So, others would think
We were happy
The vacations full of chaos
And bitter scorning
I smiled
I said, it was fun
It was tiring
The happy, quiet moments
Were with my children and
Myself
We were sabotaged
Every step of the way
Working and going to school
And raising my children
But there was just us
And a stranger
Who came in and screamed,
Demanded and used
They thought I was happy!

THE PRAYER BOXES

I went shopping
To buy a card
For two men in
Our small group
My daughter was
With me
She brought me
Over to the
Prayer Boxes
She wanted me to
Buy them for you
She explained
Each prayer box
Has three guardian angels
In them
That will guide over you
She insisted I
Buy them for you
She was excited to
See you open them
But...
You took these gifts
The wrong way
An innocent, giving child
Gave them to you
You shunned us
Gossiped about us
And hurt us very badly
You treated my daughter
Cold heartedly
Now, years later
I wonder...

Do you have the
Prayer Boxes?
My daughter doesn't
Like to come to the
Church anymore
For your fake smiles
And hugs...
Were seen by her
She was not welcomed
In the church her cousins,
Aunts and Uncles went to
I wonder...
Do you get it?
We were hurting when
We came to this church
We came for Sanctuary
To heal
Around Family
You deceived us
My daughter
She felt the betrayal
When you look at
Your Prayer Boxes
I hope you see
My daughter
I hope you understand
The power of
Love and understanding
That God gifts us
Resides in you
To my daughter
You are not
True Hearts
Of God
Remember that

6

The next time
You see her
Remember...
The Prayer Boxes
The act of Love
That was denied

THE WIDOW'S MITE

She comes each week
She is oh...so...meek
Quietly the offering plate
Passes her by
People stare
Because she can't compare
To their lofty sighs
She gently sets her
Coin into the bag
And says a little prayer
She comes each week
She is oh...so...meek
Her dress has got a tear
She sits in the back
She smiles and hugs
When the offering bag
Passes her by
She gently sets in her coin
And says a little prayer
She comes each week
She is oh...so...meek
Others stop and stare
No one sits there next to her
No one comes to greet her
She sits in the back
One day in the back
There is no one there
No one knows where
The widow has gone
She was there each week
She was oh...so...meek
Others stopped to stare

She always gently
Put in a coin
When the offering bag came by
Quietly she sat...
The widow is no longer there
As they walk down the street
They stop to stare
At the casket passing by
They quietly bend down
On one knee
And say a little prayer
For the lady who came
Each week
Who was oh...so...meek.

MY EYES WERE RAINING TODAY

My eyes were raining today
I couldn't turn off the faucet
So much hurt and pain
I've carried around
Came flooding out
I couldn't stop it
The clouds in my eyes
Finally burst
God held me tightly
Today the tears
They came down
Like rain
I couldn't stop them
He comforts me
He tries to bring
Love my way
Today...
All of the hurt and pain
Came down like rain
God wants me to let go
And look for the rainbows
The past is over
Many happy days
Are ahead
I dry my eyes
I try to smile
I try to hide
The redness in my eyes
God is here
With the angels
Comforting me and
Helping me to see

The beauty of today
I hear the birds outside
And look up to the
Blue sky and sunshine
God comforts me.

THE SEED IN MY HEART

The seed in my heart
Is starting to grow
How fast and furious
Nobody knows
But deep within my heart
My Savior picked me
To plant an extraordinary seed
Now that it is nourished
It is beginning to grow
My Savior is here
Helping to sow
For when I reap
Its beautiful gifts
The world will know
Just how deep
In love with me
My Savior can be

CINDERELLA

Cinderella your dreams
Are just around
The corner
No longer do you
Stand in
The ashes
The sunlight
Sparkles in
Your deep blue eyes
Cinderella
No longer
Is your heart
Heavy
Beauty surrounds you
And Prince Charming
Will arrive
Anytime
Cinderella
God has not
Forgotten you
He has watched
Over this jewel
In the most
Unlikely place
Now, He polishes you
And shows you
To the world
Cinderella
Joy, love and laughter
Are gifts God
Has in store for you
Cinderella

Let your wings
Take flight
You are a
Beauty to behold!

BLOSSOMS OF SPRING

Blossoms of Spring
Are in the air
Worries and fears
Have subsided
Strength in your
Heart and soul
Come from the Lord
Bluebirds will soon
Smile and flutter at
Your window
Friends and neighbors
Will hug your family
Strength of the Lord
Will fill the church
And propel it forward
On a firm foundation
Flowers will bloom
Their fragrance like
No others
Peace and Love
Will consume your life
For Spring is a new beginning!

Gina © 2 '24

HOW WISE IS THE LORD

(song)

How wise is the Lord
In all things possible
How wise is the Lord
In all things possible
He makes the sun shine
Each day
In all things possible
He makes the clouds
Go away
He makes all things possible
He makes your heart
Find the way
He makes all things possible
He makes a sunshiny day
Out of a gloomy day
He makes all things possible
He makes the moon and the stars
He makes all things possible
How wise is the Lord
He makes all things possible
How wise is the Lord
He makes all things possible
He loves you each day
He makes all things possible
So let your blues fade away
He makes all things possible
How wise is my Lord
He makes all things possible
So, Love Him each day
He makes all things possible
Let your heart

Sing His name
He makes all things possible
We pray and we pray
He makes all things possible
He loves you each day
He makes all things possible
So be happy and pray
He makes all things possible
He brings the sunshine each day
He makes all things possible
We pray and we pray
He makes all things possible
Be joyful each day
For the Lord
Loves you in
Only His way
He makes all things possible!

LOVE IS ALL AROUND YOU

Love is all around you
See the people
Taking care of one another
See the children
Laughing and smiling
Love is all around you
Lift up your heart
I am shining
A light down to show
You the way
Open the door
Let your spirit soar
Love...
Is all around you!

CHAPTER TWO

Beautiful Women

Sometimes God shows us his dreams for us, and we can't believe it. We never had such big dreams. But God has big dreams for us. He gives us hope. He is our hope. Without him things can seem impossible! God nurtures and guides us. "Beautiful Women" was a poem Jesus gave me to let me know I was beautiful and worthy. He wanted me to know that to be beautiful comes from within and that a woman can stand strong in his light.

One of the first poems Jesus gave me was "Dreams". He wanted me to know that dreams are not out of reach. They are within our reach when Jesus walks with us. "Ten Impossible Things" I wrote when Jesus walked me through his healing. He said look back and write down ten impossible things in your life since I picked you up in the midst of the wreckage.

I didn't believe I could stand strong. I had been steadying the boat and carrying the heart ache so long I didn't think I had much strength left. But Jesus showed me how to let go and stand strong through his teachings. It doesn't mean trouble will not come. Now, I stand stronger and don't cry or get upset over trials in front of me. I turn to him, and he shows me the path I must take. He gave me the poem "Today" to encourage me that he has been shaping me and I am standing stronger and wiser now.

Women are beautiful and can stand strong in this world. Jesus is here to help all of us. Women can have impossible dreams. Women can have true love in this world.

Psalms 35: 1-2: "1Plead my cause, O LORD, with them that
strive with me: fight against them that fight against me.
2Take hold of shield and buckler, and stand up for mine help" KJV

Gina©
2 '24

BEAUTIFUL WOMEN

Beautiful women
Beautiful hearts
Follow your dreams
Believe you are smart
Lean into me
As I bring you
On your way
To live a life of
Nurturing and love
In a most extraordinary way
Loving and tender
Created to care
Full of compassion and love
To those everywhere
Keep your heart
Close to mine
And you will be fine
Trust what you
Have been taught
Believe all that
I have brought to you
Be kind and loving
Cuddle and hug
Show tenderness and caring
Bring to me all of your
Strife
I will protect you and
Guide you
Throughout your life
Stand strong in the Lord
And be shiny and bright
In the Love and the caring

And all will be right
When times are challenging
Believe
I am still right here
Believe in my
Promises
And I will hold you
Each night
Lay your worries
On my shoulders
Kiss your little ones
Goodnight
Today's strife's are over
And tomorrow brings
New life
Be happy and gay
Enjoy each day
Until the day that
We meet in
The garden of life
Smell the roses
Hug and smile
Enjoy your gift of Life!

DREAMS

Hold on to me
Hold onto your dreams
Sweetly rest and
Listen as the
Angels sing
A blessed, holy lullaby
Dream my child
Of great things
Beyond your imagination
Believe in all that is
Beyond possibility
Hold onto me
Hold onto your dreams
Sleep in my arms, my child
For I am always with you
Snuggle up, lean into me
Dream of lovely, happy and joyous
Times to be
Your heart is full of a
Tremendous capacity to Love
Open it wide
Let the past be laid aside
I love you, my child
All of your dreams are
About to come true
Hold onto my hand
I will walk with you
Throughout this land
From the sand by the sea
To the heights of the mountains
Look out and believe
All that I have promised

Is meant to be
Now rest,
In your Father's arms
My child
Lovely dreams await you
Filled with Prince Charming and
A white dress
Beautiful bundles of joy
For all is yours
Rest and dream....

Ten Impossible Things

1. My children and I are happy
2. My daughter is going to college with academic scholarships
3. God just handed me the team leadership
4. God has touched me
5. God is revealing truths and changing hearts
6. My daughter is still dancing
7. My children and I are growing closer together as a family
8. Jena is graduating and a party is being arranged
9. I survived the storm through God and His Angels
10. I am loved by another

THE WOMEN

Today you invited me
To your small group
Today you decided
You would
Just be kind
Today you invited me
To share in your
Walk with God
Today you invited me
It has been so long
Since you cared or
Even gave me a nod
Today you invited me
To your little club
I have been longing
To be friends with you
But the stones you threw
Were **<u>real!</u>**
They hurt me and my family
They took away our trust
Today you invited me
To your small group
I want to believe in you
I want to trust again
But the wounds are
Still healing and
You still are trying
To put me in a box
For God so loved
The world
He gave his only
Begotten son

So, we may Love and
Care for each other
In trust and honesty
Today you invited me
To join you with
God's son and
Pray for those
Who are hurting...
But my journey has
Just begun
Healing takes a while
When the pain inflicted
Was so deep
Today you invited me
To your small group
For I want to trust you
But...
I need to forgive you and
My healing has just begun
Today you invited me
To walk with you in
Faith
But the Father,
He is guiding me
To learn to trust again
I forgive you
But your sincerity
Is just not that
Clear today...
Today you invited me
To your small group
My God, He knows
The way
Someday I will
Believe in you and

All I will say is...
Thank you for inviting me
I accept your
Invitation...
       Today!

Gina ©
2 '24

BLESSED BE...

Blessed be …
The name of the Lord
Blessed be…
The children
Whose hearts are
Innocent at birth
Blessed be…
The Mothers
Who struggle to
Protect and guide
Their children
Blessed be…
The men
Whose hearts are
Full of love and compassion
For their families
Blessed be…
The wanderers
Who seek the truths
Of the Lord
Blessed be…
The downtrodden
Where life has
Bitten and crushed
Their hearts into pieces
May they know
The miracles of the Lord
Blessed be…
The elderly and afflicted
May they know
The loving kindness of the Lord
Blessed be…

The spiritual leaders
Of the world
May they always
Seek the council of the Lord
May they follow His guidance
Above all men
Blessed be…
The poor man
For he will see
Many of the riches of heaven
Blessed be…
The outcast
For their hearts will always be
Kept close to the Father
For He walked the earth
As a friend and
An outcast
Blessed be…
The preachers
May their conscious and regard
Be those of the works of the Lord
Blessed be…
    Blessed be…
        Blessed be…
            The name…
                Of the Lord!

TODAY

Today I find a beauty
Mature and wise
Today I find a mother
Who has overcome
Great demise
Today I have an Angel
Right in front of me
For she could have
Had her vengeance
And chastised thee
Today I saw a
Christian woman
Stand, Oh, so strong
Protecting her family
From great harm
Today I saw a soldier
For the army of God
Holding up her shield
And fending off great harm
Today I witnessed a miracle
For my daughter
Has recognized me
She walks with me
In silence
For all of the world to see
Today is just the beginning
Of a wonderful life
For thee
For today I witnessed
A miracle
Thou has chosen me!

Gino© Z '24

A FREE SPIRIT

You were so beautiful
And lovely
Your smile touched
Many strangers
Your heart was a
Free spirit
Full of love
You were a blessing
To everyone you met
You encouraged others
To enjoy the life
They have been given
You were not famous
You were not rich
You made things
Happen to shine
A light on others
You should have
Never shed a tear
You were worthy of
Great love and kindness
You were a precious
beauty
One your family
Could be proud of
Your memory and legacy
Is that you showed
The world...love
May you always walk
In God's heavenly garden
In peace
Now, my beautiful
Angel of God
You will never
Shed another tear....

CHAPTER THREE

The Color Line

Jesus has been protecting me from adversity caused because I stopped to help my True Love. He is African American, and I am Caucasian. We fell in love with each other. But it was not accepted because I didn't see the color line in my hometown. My mother always wrote in the newspaper opinion page. She was always upset about something with the city or the school district. I wrote "I Crossed the Color Line" about falling in love and not being accepted because I didn't see the racial hatred still existed. Ever since I can remember racial integration was taught. I also knew my father grew up in Canada where there was racial equality. He didn't like what happened here in the USA. There is a story in our family that my father, while wearing his US uniform was threatened to be kicked off a bus in Georgia because he offered a black woman his seat. He told the bus driver that in his country no matter what a person's color a man always offers a seat to a woman. Everything I learned about racial equality is a lie. I grew up in this city. I knew the administrators in my neighborhood. My third-grade teacher was African American. I thought she was pretty and nice. That year one of the Caucasian students committed suicide by hanging himself. She cried and was very upset. She attended the funeral. She was an example to me that no matter what color we are we should care about one another. I wrote "The Color Line" because I wanted my true love to know I saw his heart, his love first. Jesus wants us to love. This is not color blindness. This is love based on two true hearts.

Sometimes when we are faced with heart wrenching truths or adversity, we become angry because of the circumstances surrounding us. Jesus taught me to walk away in silence. This doesn't mean I am conceding but sometimes our silence can speak louder than words. He gave me "Walk Away" to help me to remember this.

I wrote "Mothers" to describe how strong and resilient they are. I want women to know they are stronger than they think.

I wrote "The Red Pen" because my True Love first sent me cards and letters in red ink. After we were apart God put the red pen in my hand, writing poetry. He gave me a voice.

> *Psalms 59: 16-17: 16 "But I will sing of thy power; yea, I will sing aloud of thy mercy in the morning: for thou hast been my defence and refuge in the day of my trouble. 17 Unto thee, O my strength, will I sing: for God is my defence, and the God of my mercy." KJV*

I CROSSED THE COLOR LINE

I crossed the color line
I didn't see it
I only saw love
I embraced it
I saw the eyes of
My True Love
Starring back at me
He blushed
And smiled at me
I crossed the color line
I didn't see it
I only saw love
I embraced it
I smiled back
Blushed and gazed down
My heart felt
Alive
You stood close
You asked me
To hold your hand
I gave it in Love
I crossed the color line
I didn't see it
I only saw love
I embraced it
You asked me for help
You were weary
You seemed upset
You turned to me
I gave you help
We talked and we
Hugged

You respected me
I found a friend
Who cared about me
I crossed the color line
I didn't see it
I only saw love
I embraced it
You betrayed me
But I promised
A promise of Love
My heart hurt
I had to close a door
I never stopped loving
I never stopped praying
I had to stand up
For you didn't stand up
For me
You silenced me
You watched
When they hurt me
But I kept a promise
I walked silently
I crossed the color line
I didn't see it
I only saw love
I embraced it
God intervened
He showed us each
The truth of our hearts
He showed me
You turned around
You began following Him
I told you of His love
I told you of His forgiveness
I crossed the color line

I didn't see it
I only saw love
I embraced it
You showed me the color line
You showed me the denial
I didn't want to see it
For all that was taught me
Would be a lie
I crossed the color line
I didn't see it
I only saw love
I embraced it
I kept my promises
They were very hard
To keep
God carried me
Throughout it all
He taught and healed me
Today I stand strong
There are those who
Keep showing me
The color line
But I don't want
To see it
I crossed the color line
I didn't see it
I only saw love
I embraced it
Now God walks with me
In peace and calm
He teaches me
Many lessons
He promises me
You Love, Me
That you will keep

Your Promises
I crossed the color line
I didn't see it
I only saw Love
I Embraced It!

WALK AWAY

Walk away
When others pursue you
To chastise you
Your silence speaks
Louder than words
Walk away
When your heart
Becomes angry
Give your frustrations
To the Lord
He will deliver you
Walk away
When others want
The last word
Although they spoke
Loudly and adamantly
Your silence was the biggest
Words of all
Walk away
From those who
Belittle you
Give them no
Satisfaction of rebuttal
Walk in Peace
The silence
Frustrates them
Walk away
When jealous people
Need to tell you
What they really think
Your silence and peace
Leave them no mercy

God is the only one
Who judges you
Take heart in His love
Have faith
He will never fail you
Walk away
To your Father's arms
His armor and shield
Will always protect you
Walk away

GENTLY

(song)
Gently lay your head
Right here
Gently lay your head
Oh, so near
Gently close your eyes
For I have a surprise
Gently quiet your fears
For your beloved Father is here
Gently lean into His arms
He wants to hug you tight
Gently, my child, gently
Feel the warmth inside
Now close your eyes
Quiet your fears
For your Father's here
He gently holds you as
You fall off to sleep
Gently His hand
Caresses your brow
Lay your fears right here
Gently, my child, gently
For your Father is right here

MY CHILD, MY CHILD

My child don't be disheartened
By the stumbling of today
Don't give up, don't cry
For I will dry your eyes
A little longer is just
All I ask
My child you are lovely
My child you are worthy
So, hold on just
A little longer
For I am working diligently
Day and night
Hold on! Hold on!
I pray for you to
Hold on!
Both day and night
For beautiful daughter
I am revealing many truths
I shall bring them
To their knees
For they have hurt you and
Despised you
Just for
Believing in ME!

Gina©
2 '24

MOTHERS

Compassionate and loving
Endearing and steadfast
Guiding, enlightening
Resilient, pleasant
Secure in a compelling nature
Mothers endure life's
Ups and downs
They create a safe haven
To nurture their young
Unending Love
Caring for lives simple tasks
That the rest of the world
Ignores
Appreciating the
Turning of time
Capturing memories of
A lifetime
Mothers

A Last Goodbye

You and I were close
Our love was always there
I committed to you
But as time would tell
You never committed to me
Until I was gone
All the wrangling and
The hurt I harbored
Deep inside
Why wasn't I ever enough?
I changed and gave until…
There was nothing left
Of me …. anymore
I didn't smile
I forgot to laugh
I stopped feeling
Just let time move forward
After I was gone
You realized
It was me
You loved
You realized
All we had and built
Was between the two of us
But we were a house divided
He says, "A house divided
Will not stand!"
And in the end
It appeared to everyone else
We were strong together
But, from the beginning
I didn't know

We were a house divided
A love that could have been
So beautiful and rich
Never had a chance
In the end
You loved me and
I loved you
We have come together
And spoken our peace
In His light
Because I always knew
We both had a heart for God
Now you are with Him
I must go on here
And share my love with
Someone who loves me
Endlessly
You are healed and with God
I know we were close
I know you loved me
You are finally at peace
I go on to do God's will
I go on to Love again
We've had our last ... goodbye....

THE RED PEN

Letters arrived and cards
With red ink
"You are a good Mom"
"I Love You…Always"
Every note you wrote me
In red ink
I began sending poems
In red ink
One after another
I was falling
In love with you
Then a devastating hurt
Arrived
It was confusing
Down deep I was
Distraught
No more red ink
Cards or letters
A very dark time for me
I tossed and turned
Struggling to understand
The nightmare before me
God kept showing me
My promise
Through it all
Suddenly the poems
Began to come
Through me again
One day I realized
The red pen
Was in my hand
Writing poems

Words from God
To share with others
Who go through
Life's trials
The Red Pen
A Love Letter
Between ME and God!

HUGS

A hug of kindness
A hug of peace
A hug of comfort
A hug of possession
A hug of appearances
Just for others to see
A hug of friendship
A hug of compassion
A hug of sympathy
A hug of nurturing
A hug of forbidden love
Hidden where no one can see
A hug of hello
A hug of goodbye
A hug of fellowship
A hug of joy
A hug of two hearts
Never to part

HEARTS

A heart for God
True and unfailing
A kind, open
Generous heart
Always there to Love
And show compassion
A heart of mercy and forgiveness
One that doesn't pass
Judgement
A heart that's calm and
Nurturing
One that wraps its love
Around you
A heart that endures
The test of time
Yet remains deep in
Love for others
Hearts

WALKING WITH GOD

Today I walked with God
He showed me love
And compassion
Today a man stood
At the side of the road
Begging for money
It was cold and
Freezing rain
He was dressed warm
But he wouldn't be there
If he had a home
Today I walked with God
I stopped and
Signaled him to come
Over to my car
I gave him some money
He said, "God Bless You"
I said, "Stay warm"
God has already
Blessed me
Today he let me
Bless someone else
Today God walked
With me
He showed me
The man
Whose truck skidded
Into the ravine
I wondered if he
Was alright
I passed him by
God brought someone

To help him
Today I walked with God
I saw a woman
Stranded in a ravine
On the other side
Of the road
I wondered if
She was okay
God brought her help
Today God walked
With me
The sheriff at the
Court house entry
Gave me directions
To my appointment
Today God walked
With me
I met the lady
Who helped me
On the phone
She was kind and
Helped me with
My DBA
I thanked her for
Being so kind
On the phone
Today God walked
With me
I was grateful my
Children were safe
In this weather
He helped me realize
I forgot something
Today God walks
With me

I am grateful to
Know him and
How close he walks
With me
Today, God showed me
Love
Compassion
Patience
And Peace
I am Blessed
For my Savior
Walks close to me

Chapter Four

Promises

The world can seem small or enormous depending on your perceptions and experiences in the world. Jesus is "Working all Around Us" changing the world for good. We are so busy running here and there that we fail to see his presence. Jesus taught me to slow down and to quiet my mind so I could see his works all around me.

I love music. It is a part of who I am. It helps me when I am low, it lifts me up. Music makes me happy. I appreciate the talents of others and question Jesus what it all means in my life. I think the arts are an essential part of everyone's education. I encouraged both of my children to participate in band at school. On my journey with them I met different band teachers. I admire them. When I think about my children starting in third grade and progressing into high school, I think of what angel's band teachers must be. I wrote "The Band Teacher" from my experiences as a parent of a band student.

I have worked with children under the age of seven for all my career. I love their spirit and energy. When I was young, I found it was important to have a song in your heart. It helps you shine. When my children were little, I had a playroom for them. I liked coming home from work and just sit and play with them. Sometimes I would sit and watch them from another room playing and pretending. It is inspirational. At work I loved sitting and playing with the children and helping them discover new things. I wrote, "If You Could See Through a Child's Eyes", reflecting on those times.

My True Love doesn't know how important he is to me. He doesn't understand he was in my life for a reason. For, I was lost and alone, trying to find a way to stand up strong. It was his love for me that made me feel wanted and loved. It gave me the courage to stand up strong and change the course of my life. I walked away from him so I could decide the course without being confused about my feelings. He was my confidant. He doesn't know that no harm came to me and my children because no one knew what I knew. They didn't know how much of the truths about my ex-husband I knew. This kept us safe. This is something God did. I wrote "If Not for You" to tell him God used him to help keep us safe. I will always love him for this.

I promised a promise of love to my True Love. I explained to him I would never hate him that I would always love him, because he opened his heart to me during a dark time in my life. He made me feel loved and worthy. It gave me the strength to stand up for my children's future. I have kept that promise. I wrote promises because Jesus promised never to forsake us, and he has never wavered for me. I am blessed.

Psalms 10: 17-18: 17" LORD, thou hast heard the desire of the humble: thou wilt prepare their heart, thou wilt cause thine ear to hear: 18 To judge the fatherless and the oppressed, that the man of the earth may no more oppress."

You are Working All Around Us

You are working all around us
I see it
Like I've never seen
It before
I listen in the
Quiet
I stand in the
Silence
A witness of your
Mighty hand
At work
Changing the world
For good
Perceptions of people
Are so small
They miss your
Presence
Right under their
Noses
I stand in the distance
In the silence
I see your hand
Creating and changing
Lives
People don't see the
Big picture
They are in such a
Hurry
They miss the
Grand things you do
You are working
All around us

Gina © 2 '24

THE SOUNDS OF NATURE

Chirping, croaking, buzzing
Singing sweet songs of praise
Squawking, cooing, whistling
Waking up the day
Twitter, twirl. Whipple whirl
Calling friends to come
Out to play
Singing high, singing low
Singing softly, singing loudly,
Nestled high in the trees
Nurturing their young babies
Busy, whizzing to and fro
Working 'til the sun sets low
Softly, sweetly lulls the day
In the evening
New friends come
Out to play
In the darkness
Under the moonlight
Where the stars shine
Very bright
Hooting, squeaking, howling
Swooning high, swooping low
Nocturnal friends
Delight the night
Playing hide and seek
While others are fast asleep.

Gina©
2 '24

MUSIC

Music surrounds me
It makes me
Smile inside
Music wipes my
Cares away
Music is my love song
Between God
And myself
Music makes me
Want to spread
My wings
And fly
Don't try to catch me
When I am soaring so high
Music helps me shed
My cares away
Music is so sweet
When it lulls
A baby to sleep
Music is in my
Heart and soul
It helped me
Climb Mountains
And sail the seas
It brings me closer
To thee
Music surrounds me
It brings laughter and tears
Music helps me
Live a full life
Music is all around me
Even when my heart
Skips a beat

SING WITH THE ANGELS

Sing with the Angels
All of my love
Sing with the Angels
From your heart
Look up above
Sing with the Angels
Let your beautiful voice
Be heard
Sing with the Angels
All of the days
Of your life
Sing with the Angels
There will be no strife
For I am with you
Sing with the Angels
My beautiful child
Sing with the Angels
Until the days
Where you will return
To this place
Sing, sing with the Angels
My beautiful child

Gina©
2 '24

THE BAND TEACHER

The band teacher
Is an unusual
Character
He must be…
All those notes
He has to labor over
Perfection is in his heart
But many wonder
Does he know
Good music
How can he stand up
In front of
All those people
So professional
So accurate
When the notes
Come blaring out
Like a piano
Needing to be tuned
He stands there
So, assured.
That what he is
Listening to
Is beautiful and lovely
The band teacher
An unusual character
He must have
Cotton in his ears
When he stands
In front of his audience
He has a belief
In perfection

And faith in
Children's talents
The band teacher
Must be an Angel
To put all of those
Awkward notes together
To make musicians
Out of little children

IF YOU COULD SEE THROUGH A CHILD'S EYES

If you could see through a child's eyes
What wonder and amazement
You would see
A world of possibilities
A world of beginnings
Everything fresh
Everything new
If you could see through a child's eyes
Nothing could hurt you
There would be no pain
For the future is filled with
Excitement, adventures, and change
If you could see through a child's eyes
What love would surround you
All the beautiful things
God created
Would touch your heart

IF NOT FOR YOU

If not for you
Entering into my life…
I wouldn't feel beautiful again
If not for you
My children wouldn't
Feel safe and secure
If not for you
There would be no
Loving tuck-ins
If not for you
I wouldn't feel
Safe in my home
If not for you
I wouldn't see a future
Filled with hopes and dreams
If not for you
I wouldn't have asked God
To help me turn my life around
If not for you
I wouldn't appreciate my father.
If not for you
Touching my life
Touching my heart
My new friends
And neighbors
Wouldn't have come
Into my life
I always knew
That when you touch a life
You affect that life
For good or for bad
Sometimes we hurt

Those who are closest to us
But one act cannot erase
The good in a person
And the love they touched
You with
Their heart
You felt
Their dreams you
Listened to
Their trials
you stood by
Them through
If not for you...
I wouldn't be stronger
Wiser and caring
Though some of what happened
Hurts deeply
Though I struggle to understand
Everything
The whys...
Deep in my heart
I have love for you
Nothing can change that
God showed me the
Loving, caring side of you first
If not for you...
My life may have ended
Although I am struggling emotionally
Right now
I know God is with me
I know I will
Love you always
I know that when you love someone
You want the best for them
I wish you love and peace...

GOD LOVES ME

God loves me
He touches my
Heart everyday
From out of the blue
A smile and a hug
The sound of laughter
The voice of a
Tiny tot welcoming me
Yes, God Love Me
He caresses my soul
He soothes my fears
Everyday a new blessing
Is revealed and my
Perceptions are shown
To be false
Oh, My God
How He Loves Me!
With a grateful heart
I thank Him
For each day and everyday
I can breathe out and breathe in
And when that
Enormous Mountain appears
Right before my eyes
He walks me through it
And as I turn to say
Goodbye
He gives me His love
And strength
To see the hopes and beauty
Of tomorrow
Yes, How My God Loves Me
When I am doubtful
And fear fills my day

A smile of a loved one
Makes it all go away
When I am in
Darkness
When there is no end
In sight
He holds me tight
He tells me He will
Never forsake me
Through the dark nights
When the sun arises
He sends me
Bright light
And shows me the
Darkness is far
Out of sight
Oh Yes,
My God, He Loves Me
And I sit and wonder
Why
In His garden
Beside Him as
He reveals all of the lies
My God, He Loves ME
I'll never understand
The depth of His wisdom
The mercy of His grace
But
I am somebody
Because...
My God,
He
Loves
Me
For
Eternity!

I'll Remember You in a Dream

I Love you
I'll remember you
In a dream
Somewhere
I'll hold you
I'll kiss you
Good and tight
I'll love you
I'll remember you
In a dream
Somewhere
I'll take care of you
I'll Love you
I'll hold you
I'll remember you
In a dream
Somewhere
I need you
I want you
I'll take care of you
I'll remember you
In a dream
Somewhere
I'll be with you
I'll kiss you
I'll hold you
Good and tight
I'll Love you
I'll remember you
In a dream
Somewhere

Gina© 2 '24

SOMETHING IN THE WAY YOU SMILE

Something in the way you
Smile
Lights up my heart
Something in the way you
Draw close to me
Makes me feel loved
Something in the way you
Hold me
Makes me feel like a
Fragile piece of China
Something in the way you
Gaze at me across a room
Let's me know
I am in your heart
Something in the way you
Hold my hand
Makes me feel that you
Want me in your life
Something in the way you
Try to get my attention
Tells me I am your
True Love
Something in the
Twinkle in your eyes
Makes me smile and
Tell you... I Love you!

HE IS LIKE...

He is like...
The morning sun
Shining brightly
Through your heart
He lights it on fire
With compassion
He compels you to
Touch other's lives
He compels you to
Rescue and care
For the wounded
Of the world
He is like...
The morning dew
Refreshing your spirit
When the world has
Taken you through
A storm
He is like...
The peacefulness
On a quiet summer morning
When a gentle breeze
Touches you and
Wraps you in His love
He is like...
The candle that lights up
The night
Watching over you
So that you are
Safe and sound
He is there
In the quiet

As you fall
Off to sleep
Soothing the fears
You have gathered
Throughout the day
He is like...
The winding stream
He stays with you
Through all of the
Twists and turns
He is like...
A waterfall
Pouring the
Water of Life
Over you to keep you
Safe and persevering
He is like...
A Majestic Mountain
Standing mighty and strong
Never wavering in
His love for you
You are His and
He will fight for you
Just lean into Him
He is like
The ocean
Vast in His
Love for you
He is never leaving.

TODAY AND EVERY DAY

Today and every day
Say a prayer
Believe you are here
To walk with me
Today and every day
Take a moment
To look around
I hear your prayer
Take a glimpse of
The beauty that
Surrounds you
Take a picture
Keep it in your heart
Today and every day
Sing with joy from
Deep within you
Lift up your voice
For all to hear
I am shaping you
Do not be afraid of
Those who might
Stop and stare
Today and every day
Believe I walk with you
Take notice of the needy
Share and love
Show deep compassion
I am with you always
Today and every day
Lay down and rest
Pick up the memories
You remember best

Settle in snuggly and
As you fall off to
Sleep
Listen…Listen…
To the Angels singing
While I watch you sleep.

PROMISES

The sun is setting
Everything is serene
The hopes and dreams
For tomorrow will soon
Be spinning in your head
Hopes of happier tomorrows
Dreams of fairy tales,
Kings and Queens and
The saving Knight
But when you awake
You'll find you are
The one God picked
To slay the Giants
By walking close to Him
And on a beautiful day
You will turn your head
And smile
For your Prince Charming
Will be standing at your door
Expressing his unending love
For you
On this day
All of the struggles
Fears and strife will
Seem far away
Joy and Love
Will fill your heart
And I will lift you high
He will stand beside you
And never waiver
For in the end
I made both of you

To journey this world
To find one another
And unfold
Beautiful miracles of my
Amazing Grace.

AN OPEN HEART TO GOD

An open heart to God
Is just the start
Of a beautiful life
Without any strife
An open heart to God
Keeps you safe and warm
The adversaries will
Be set to rest
The trouble will end
An open heart to God
Is pure and unselfish
It is most lovely
It shines bright
Even in the night
An open heart to God
Is very precious
To Him
His grace will cover you
His love will comfort you
Even through
The darkest storms
For an open heart to God
Is all a Father can ask for
From His children
The center of that heart is
Pure Love
And
Love is the...
             Center of ...
                  All Things!

Gina©
2 '24

FORGIVENESS

God has taught me a
Better way to forgive
A way that I can
Stand strong and not be
Taken advantage of
I have been hurt, deeply
By many others
He has been
Helping me
To guard my heart and
Stand strong
He knows of the
Injustices
But most of their lives
Have moved on
He walks me out
Of the ashes today
He asks me to
Lay down the
Hurt and pain
I have accumulated
Over many years
He asks me to
Forgive
Let go…
And love
It has been hard
For I trust
Only in him
He tells me it's okay
I am safe now
He is justifying me

From all of the wrongs
It's time to
Let go and
Live again
Today I have
Forgiven
All of those who
Have hurt me and
My family
Today I am at
Peace
He is here
He is holding me tightly
He is justifying me
Today I have…
Forgiven.

SITTING HERE IN THE QUIET

Sitting here in the quiet
Talking to you
Knowing you are here
To catch me when
I stumble and fall
Sitting here in the quiet
With you holding my hand
Renders a security
I do not understand
Sitting here in the quiet
Where I am
Nurtured and loved
Keeps me calm
Helps me see hope
When I am in
Your arms
Sitting here in the quiet
Waiting for my True Love
To come
My Father sits
Teaching me and
Showing me the
Things that are to come
Sitting here in the quiet
I know all that
I've done
Is not in vain
And the truth
Will come
Sitting here in the quiet
In God's holy place
There is no
Destruction
There is only…
                    Grace

CATCHING BLESSINGS FROM ABOVE

Blessings of the world
Come from God
He throws blessings
Down from heaven
For you to catch and
Share with others
Blessing's cascade
Down from heaven
Like snowflakes in the
Blue sky
Blessings from God
Melt and evaporate if
We don't stop to
Catch them
We are so busy
Looking down
Planning every step
Before we take it
We forget to
Look up,
Look around and
Catch the
Blessings from...
                    Above!

CHAPTER FIVE

God Sees All

We are all God's people. He ignites our spirit and brings us to higher heights in our lives through our interactions with one another. I wrote "Our Spiritual Light" to describe this, when God ignites our spirit, it lights a way for others to follow him.

On my journey with God, he keeps teaching me patience. I wrote "Patience" after experiencing the many lessons he has taught me with patience. Our impatience can interfere with what God is doing. Sometimes, we have to wait on God. It helps bring us peace.

My True Love asked me for help when his father was dying. He would ask me questions about relationships and love. I told him to talk to his father about this. One of the few times we were together he was hurting because his father's health was deteriorating. I wrote "Sitting in the Silence" about him and his Father during the time he was taking care of his Father.

In the end we think we are in charge and taking things into our own hands. But this is not true. God is in charge, "God Sees All"!

Psalms 45: 17: "I will make thy name to be remembered in all generations: therefore shall the people praise thee for ever and ever." KJV

DWELLING HOUSE

I shall rest
In the
Dwelling House
Of the Lord
Through Him
All things come
He holds me close
Restful and Peaceful
He sings to me
His words
Strong and Steady
He teaches me
To walk
I shall rest
In the
Dwelling House
Of the Lord
He teaches me how to walk
And do great things
For He walks
Beside me
I shall rest
In the
Dwelling House
Of the Lord
Calm and Serene
My heart is content
I see
Great things
For the Lord
Needs my help
He stands in

My presence and
Guides my heart
Everything shall
Come to be
For it is His
Will for me
I am loved deeply
By my Father
I shall rest
In the Dwelling House
Of the Lord
The rest of my life
He keeps me
Safe and sound
My head does not
Spin around
For it is His
Will for me
To do great things
In His name
I pray
I shall rest
In the
Dwelling House
Of the Lord

THE TOUCH OF YOUR HAND

I feel your hand
Reassuring me
Everything is ok
God is guiding me
And I am on my way
I feel your hand
Touching my face
When I think of
Your son and God's
Amazing Grace
You help God guide me
The love I feel
In this touch
Makes my heart warm
And I love your
Son so much
The touch of your hand
Makes me feel
I am a part of
Your family too
Your love transcends
All earthy bounds
The touch of your hand
When no one else
Is around
Makes the Dreams
Feel possible
One miracle after
Another unfolds
The touch of your hand
Sends your son's
Love my way

Tomorrow
He may appear
In such a loving way
I hope he holds my hand
So, I can feel his love
And the world will know
God brought us together
From above
The touch of your hand
Makes me feel loved
No matter what the world
May think
The touch of your hand
Is what I need
To walk this land
Until my
True Love arrives and
God's spirit soars
I am blessed from
Above
For you to show
Me such Love with
The touch of your...
Hand

SISTA'S

A common bond
Between two Sista's
Caring, sharing
Life experiences
Crying and trying
To hold each other's hands
Through life's
Stormy seas
Sista's
Strengthening one another
Letting their inner beauty
Glow outward
For others to see
Through their
Daily work of love
Joy and friendship
Carrying one another
Throughout their lifetimes
Dropping petals
Of lives simple
Lessons of
Love, laughter and
A lifetime of friendship
Sista's

THE MESSENGER

God brings me messages
Through a messenger
He brings my promise
Through His angels
He shows me lessons
Through the young children
Who hug me
God brings me messages
Through all kinds of messengers
Someone says something
It inspires a poem
The poem is a new lesson
To be learned
God brings me messages
Through messengers
Who bring Hope, Faith and Love
God brings me messengers
To light and guide my way.

Gina©
2 '24

THE HEALING

He heals the hurt
Down deep in my soul
He heals the pain
Others have inflicted on me
He heals my doubts
By showing me how
To walk in Faith
He mends the fences
Between family and friends
God is healing
My world
He heals and I see
His hand at work
Impossibilities become possible
Enemies become friends
The helpless remain protected
He unveils a beautiful world
Of warmth and love
Everything is lighter
No burdens to bear
God does the healing
I do the believing
I walk in Faith
I live for Him
Through me His Love
Is shown
He gives me Hope
God's hand does the healing.

OUR SPIRITUAL LIGHT

God sees our
Spiritual Light
God sees it shine
Brilliantly when
We do His works
And walk in the light
When we walk in
Darkness
God sees our
Brilliant Light
Grow dim
He beckons us
To turn around
He stands at the end
Of that road
Shining a brilliant
Spiritual Light
For us to turn around
And follow
He walks down that
Dark road to help
Us up and
Guides us back
To where we can
Shine brilliantly again
He forgives us
God sees our
Spiritual Light

IN THE HEART OF CHILDREN

In the heart of children
There is laughter
In the heart of children
There are hopes and dreams
In the heart of children
There is a delightful spirit
In the heart of children
There is innocence
In the heart of children
There is truth and honesty
In the heart of children
There is fairness
In the heart of children
There is love and
Compassion
In the heart of children
There is
Jesus!

Gina©
2 '24

LIVE YOUR LIFE

Live your Life
As if every day
Were your first
Live your Life
With excitement
And adventure
Dream your life
Into reality
Enjoy the smiles
Laughter and love
Collect heartwarming hugs
Endearing glances
Showering others with
God's Love
Live your Life
Like every day
Were your first

Gina©
2 '24

PATIENCE

God
Greets
Each
Person At
The Gates
Of
Heaven

Gino©
Z '24

TOUCHING LIVES

Each day each one of us
Is touching another's life
When we touch a life
We change that life
For good or for bad
When we touch a life
We change that life
So let us walk
Like He walked
Passing out petals
Of kindness, love,
Joy, peace and hope
Caring for one another
In this vast world
Of wonders
Let us sow seeds
We can cherish
For a lifetime
While Touching
One another's Lives.

Gino© 2 '24

CHILDREN SEE GOD

Children see God
In the clouds
Floating by
Children see God
In the people
They meet
Children see God
Amongst the
Dandelions
Children see God
In the baby animals
They hold
Children see God
In the wind-blown trees
Children see God
Along the long
Sandy beaches
Children see God
In the depths
Of the ocean
Children see God
Amongst the birds
In the sky
Children see God
In their
Mommies and Daddies eyes
Children see God
In the stars
Up in the immense night sky
Children see God
As they close their
Sleepy eyes

Children have
Faith, Hope and Love
In their hearts
Children see God!

AWAKENING

Blossoms peeling open
Reaching out to the sunlight
Vines winding around
In a whimsical pattern
A fresh morning dew
Quenches thirst
The sky painted with feathers
Of blue and white
A gentle breeze
Carrying petals hither and yon
New Life
Springtime!

CONTAGIOUS

When I look at their innocent faces
A contagious smile overcomes me
Looking into sparkling
Curious eyes
A contagious smile
Warms my heart
I can't be angry or sad
A delightful laughter
And a contagious giggle occurs
Babies are a gift from God
Full of wonderment
They can melt years off of your life
A simple game or peek-a-boo
A wink, a chuckle
They are full of hugs and kisses
The innocent look of a baby
Reminds us of Jesus
A gift from God
So, sing a lullaby
Snuggle and Hug
Your little ones
The Love
That radiates from them is
Contagious!

SITTING IN THE SILENCE

Sitting in the silence
Next to you
I look back at those
Many years
I see in your aged eyes
I remember the laughter
The fun
I remember how you
Taught me to walk
How you chuckled
As I showed off
My new talents
Sitting in the silence
I remember every game
You sat and watched
I remember how you
Checked me when
I was going astray
Sitting in the silence
I remember every day
You went off to work
To give me a better life
Sitting in the silence
My heart is hurting
I want to comfort you
From your pain
Sitting in the silence
I pray!

Gina© 2 '24

God Sees All

When things appear mixed up
Give all to God
For God sees all
We are just, people
With different perceptions
Of our part of the world
But God sees all
When you are troubled
And can't find your way
Give all to God
For God sees all
He cares for all of us
He unravels the twists
And turns
And knots we've created
He asks us to sit silently
And watch Him unwind
Our mess and shows us
His wondrous works
His hand is gentle
His temperament is tender
He carefully takes care
And
Nurtures all of those involved
He teaches as He toils
We stand in awe
At His wondrous works
For when He is done
He teaches us to walk
Like Him and
Love one another
For God sees all!

CHAPTER SIX

The Watchers

During the time when I was writing my poetry on tiles, I posted pictures of my tiles on my Google site. Each month I would receive a report from Google of the number of views of my pictures. At one point I reached five thousand views. God showed me that people were watching my site for new poems on tiles. I wrote the poem "The Watchers" about these people.

After my children and I were reunited we spent an evening watching a college play my daughter was in. The whole time I watched the play I enjoyed seeing how happy and joyous she was. I wrote "Today, I watched You" and "Together Again" about this evening. It was so peaceful and joyous.

The truth hurts very deeply sometimes. I wrote "I Grew Up Here" about the people who lived in my neighborhood where I grew up, who judged me and hurt me. They don't realize I know they were involved. They also don't realize the hurt and pain they're acts inflicted on my children's lives.

When I moved and began my life with my children anew, the gossip about our private family affairs, were spread in the new area I was living. At the church I attended and in the schools my children attended. I had to stand up to protect my children. After their father died, my son was taken out of soccer. My daughter was chastised at church by adults and kept from attending the summer camp the church children went to. The women who befriended me were false. They gossiped behind our backs. Throughout all of this we volunteered as a family at the church. We contributed to the Homeward Bound initiative to build a church. I wrote "Homeward Bound" about this time.

God continues to shape and guide my life. My children are adults now. They are beginning their own lives. They continue to show compassion and love for others. They have friends and family around them. The church is almost complete. I am the only one who has remained in the church because God guided me through the storm and helped me stand up to my adversaries. I wrote "Great Plans" about the church that is being built. I pray that I am welcome there.

Psalms 17: 1-5 : 1"(A Prayer of David.) Hear the
right, O LORD, attend unto my cry, give ear unto
my prayer, *that goeth* not out of feigned lips.
2Let my sentence come forth from thy presence; let
thine eyes behold the things that are equal.
3Thou hast proved mine heart; thou hast visited *me* in
the night; thou hast tried me, *and* shalt find nothing; I
am purposed *that* my mouth shall not transgress.
4Concerning the works of men, by the word of thy lips
I have kept *me from* the paths of the destroyer.
5Hold up my goings in thy paths, *that* my footsteps slip not." KJV

TWO BROTHERS

I met them
In my darkest hour
Trying to stand up
Again
One was kind and caring
One was skeptical with a
Discerning eye
They both found it in
Their hearts to take a
Chance on me and my
Daughter
They were patient
Offered a helping hand
They made sure we
Were happy here
Two brothers
Every week they stopped
To ask how we were
If we needed anything
No judgement
Very professional
But kind and friendly
They helped us feel
At home here
We lost our home
We were torn up inside
Trying to heal and trust
Again
Two brothers, steadfast
Made sure flowers were
Here in the Spring
Made sure the snow

Was cleared in the Winter
Two brothers
God touched their hearts
To help us feel at home
Here
They smiled and asked
How we are doing
They cared
When many did not
Two brothers
Humble in God's light
Working hard day in and
Day out
Helping each other
Opened their hearts
To help us
Stand up again
Two Brothers

TODAY I WATCHED YOU

Today I watched you
Full of joy and happiness
The sparkle in your eyes
Smiling so beautifully
Today you were doing
Something you loved to do
In your heart
Amongst your friends
You were so happy
I thanked God
Today I watched you
In your first play
You seemed at home
And very happy
I thanked God for
Protecting you and
Healing you
Today I watched you
And my heart leaped for
Joy
For the storm is over and
You were very happy.

TOGETHER AGAIN

Dedicated to My Children

Tonight was beautiful
We had smiles on
Our faces
We were sharing news
Of our lives with
One another
We are together again
Just enjoying
One another's company
Sharing a fun time
Enjoying just being together
We are happy tonight
To be together
We all live apart
We see each other
On occasion
But tonight
Sharing a new experience
Together
Filled our hearts
With joy
For God has brought us
Together again.

A Beautiful Day

Today is a Beautiful Day
For you are free
Your chains are broken
You are learning to
Walk anew
He is coming!
He will bring flowers
And a true heart
Today is a Beautiful Day
With the blue sky and
Sunshine
I will bring the
Bluebirds
And your True Love
Very soon
Enjoy this beautiful day
For peace is yours and
Happiness beyond compare
Is on the horizon
Yes… My daughter
Today is a Beautiful Day
Just for you!

THE WATCHERS

Today God revealed
They are watching me
I didn't see it
I thought they
Didn't care
I thought they
Were righteous
I thought their
Stones were
Still in their hands
I'm so use to trying
To protect myself
God told me to
Lay down my armor
And shield
Today God revealed
They are watching me
As I write all
Of these poems
He has given me
To help me heal
Today God is here
He has shown me
His work
Today he has shown me
The watchers
And how he is changing
Their hearts to
Walk closer to Him
These things are not
In my hands
They are in God's hands
Today God revealed
The Watchers!

MASKS

They put on their
Masks
To hide their hearts
They smile
They pretend to
Be my friend
They put on their
Masks
Making sure they are
Perfect and Pretty
They stand tall
They come close
Pretending to have
Great concern for me
But I can see
Through their masks
Their hearts
Cannot lie
They ask the same old
Questions
They act concerned
For my family
They put on their masks
And adjust them
Just right
They smile and hug
When their leader is
Present
They put on their
Masks
And fix their hair
They come without

A true heart
They stop and stare
But when their leader
Is not around
They don't know
I am here
They ignore me
They have that
Far off glare
But when he comes in
The masks go
Back on
They smile and hug
They are unaware
That Jesus has
Taught me
To recognize
Their Masks

My First Friend

You were my first friend
In this new place
You seemed kind and caring
You seemed interested
In my family
I was glad to meet a
Person who was a
Christian
In this new place
But you were not a
True friend
You were following a
Personal agenda
Trying to find out what
The gossip was all about
Every time you came up to me
You were full of jokes and silliness
You were only
Fishing for information
I did not know
You seemed interested
In helping the church rise
But you were not a friend
When my family
Lost our home
You couldn't look at me
You couldn't face me
But isn't that what you
Wanted?
You couldn't look at
My daughter
The devastation in her

Face
You couldn't see it through
We are standing again
But instead of my family
Remaining here
We are scattered
You didn't welcome us
As a family
My children cannot face
The people who said
Awful things about their
Mother
They know they are not true
I can't speak of it
Right now
The words cannot come
Just yet
But now…
I see God's work in you
He has changed your heart
Now, you are trying to
Be my friend
But that is in
God's hands
For our wounds are still fresh!

I GREW UP HERE

I grew up here
I had friends
I found love here
I ran, sang and danced here
I played baseball in the corner lot
We all played Pom! Pom!
On the corner
I grew up here
I found love
I had hopes and dreams here
I sat on the porch drawing
And dreaming
I grew up here
I knew teachers, administrators, doctors, lawyers and judges
They were my neighbors
I grew up here
There were African American, Caucasian, Indian,
Jewish, Catholic and Baptist people here
We were neighbors
I grew up here!
I got married
I had children
I got divorced
I grew up here
I moved away
I enjoyed being happy
I came back for
Thanksgiving, Christmas and Easter
I grew up here
I fell in love again here
Then a devastating betrayal
Many of my neighbors had a

Hand in it
I grew up here
The truth hurts deeply because
I grew up here!

MY FRIENDS, WHERE ARE YOU?

My friends, where are you?
I thought all of the time
We spent together was beautiful
We learned from each other
We cared and helped one another
My friends, where are you?
I've been alone for so long
I feel abandoned…alone
You and I we cared and shared
Our life's experiences
We came together to greet
Each new baby
We celebrated life
My friends, where are you?
Jesus consoles me here…alone
My friends, where are you?

HOMEWARD BOUND

Homeward Bound
Our church was saving
To build a building
Homeward Bound
God touched me
He said, "do not tithe"
"Tithe only to Homeward Bound"
I tithed each week
That I could
To Homeward Bound
When my children's father died
I contributed the last
$3,000,00 to pay off the land
Homeward Bound
Each week
I gave what I could
The church gathered
On the land
To clean up,
To talk and share
About the building plans
I came with
My two children
But...
We were not welcome
And many let us
Know this
Homeward Bound
I kept tithing
Whenever I could
Through trials
Tribulations

Happiness
Love and
Peace
I kept tithing
Our Pastor announced
Two weeks and we will
Break ground
God is bringing us
Together
Homeward Bound

GREAT PLANS

Out in the country
Down a winding dirt road
Lies a section of land
So beautiful and quiet
The trees are many
You can hear the birds
Singing, "Hallelujah"
Out in the country
Down a winding dirt road
Where life is simple
There is no traffic
To control
Lies a piece of land
Purchased for my King
Great plans are unfolding
Great things are being
Revealed
In a quiet place
In the country
Where the wind and leaves
Blow
Lies a piece of land
And many Great Plans
For my Savior, he is there
Setting up his house
So that when the people
Arrive
He will shed his love and
Great Joy
He will listen for
Their voices singing
Loudly

As they proclaim
Their love for their
Savior
There will be no shame
For now, my Savior
Sits in this quiet place
Watching the sun rise and set
Listening to the animals sing
He talks with his Father
About many Great Things
He is preparing a house
For his people
To worship and share
His love with
One another
Throughout this land
My Savior is sitting
Quietly
Today
As he prays to
His Father
Of Great Things
To come…

          Someday.

THE BEAUTIFUL LIFE

Born an innocent baby
In unusual circumstances
Held by the most
Beloved Mother
He came
A present to the world
No one thought
He should not have come
He spread joy and hope
Throughout the world
Upon His arrival
One bright star in the sky
He came
He was so innocent
But He blossomed and thrived
No fame, no fortune
He was
The Beautiful Life
God gave in Love.

THE KEYS

God keeps putting keys
In my hands
I don't know why
I have been given
These keys
But they are from people
Who have not trusted me
The first keys in my hands
Was a key ring of keys
I offered to hold for
Safe keeping
Until the owner was able
To come and get them
Though I offered her many
Opportunities to pick up her keys
It wasn't until 15 years later
That she retrieved her keys
Then I received a key
From work after much
Chastisement
I received two keys from
My church after false
Accusations
I received a key from
My Aunt and Uncle after they
Asked me to leave
Their home
I received another key from work
I don't need
All of these keys
But God keeps giving me
Keys

I ask God,
"What do the keys mean?"
He says;
You are loved
You are trusted
I have justified you
From lies and jealousy
You are a good person
You are trusted

THE BAPTISM

God is here
He is at the water
Offering life
New life
He asks us to
Come to the water
And thirst no more
But I came
As a baby
I've believed in Him
All of my life
Terrible hurts encompassed me
My world was changing
I was just standing strong
Then a terrible hurt hit me
I didn't see it coming
I finally had the courage
To open my heart
All of the way
To love again
It felt right
I was dumb founded
Hurt deeply
No one knew it
It was a secret
God was holding me up
I couldn't carry the secret
I came to the water
To satisfy others who
Didn't recognize my baptism
As a baby and to let go
Of the hurt

I was carrying around
I came
I was submerged
I let go of a
Heavy weight
I didn't feel different
My load just felt lighter
I like the picture
Of my second baptism
It means
I let go
I let God lead the way
I know God recognized
My first baptism
The people who
Accused me of a
Ransomed baptism
Were wrong
I know God has always
Been with me
Throughout my life
The Baptism
New Life!

SMILE

Smile to the Lord
Lift up your heart
Let joy fill your
Song
Smile for it spreads
Love and happiness
It lifts your spirit
And soothes your soul
Smile and touch a
Heart burdened with
Strife
Touch a heart
Show others how
Jesus walked
Smile
Let your soul
Shine
Smile!

LOVE YOUR NEIGHBOR

Love your neighbor
Lend a helping hand
Remind them of
The light and the love
Love your neighbor
Share caring words
And kind gestures
Believe in their
Friendship
Trust in the Lord
Listen to their grief
Love your neighbor
Offer inspirational
Thoughts
Uplift their spirit
Lend a strong shoulder
Help them stand up
Love your neighbor
Share in God's love
The spirit of hope
And Peace
From above

CHAPTER SEVEN

A Love from Above

During the time I was close to my true love I began writing poems to him. I wrote a small book of poems and gave them to him. God has revealed to me that he still has those poems. I hope someday he will come with my book of poems. I did not retain any copies of the poems. But I remember them. I wrote a poem about my father. Why would he keep that poem if he didn't know how much it means to me? I wrote "The Sand and The Stone" from a conversation we had via text on a Sunday morning. It describes how God shapes our lives. During the time I was close to my true love I began running again. I wrote a poem about this. My favorite poem is "Resting Place". He knows these poems are very close to my heart. If he didn't love me, why would he keep my poems? Sometimes, it isn't in what we say but in how we act.

This chapter is about my true love and the questions that are on my heart.

"Surely the righteous are rewarded; surely there is a
God that judges the earth." Psalms: 58:11.

Gino©
2 '24

I HAVE THIS DREAM

I have this dream
That one day
I will meet my
True Love again
He will come
With a true heart
Kneeling before me and
Professing his Love
For me
I have this dream
In my heart
Our love will transcend
Earthly perceptions of
Race and Prejudice
That we will walk in Peace
Showing the world
That God loves all of us
I have this dream
That I will walk
Hand in hand
With my True Love
Despite gossip and false
Perceptions
I will smile and love him
I will dance and laugh
With him
I have this dream
We will wed and
Many will understand
That only God
Could have brought us
Together

And that He can create
Impossible Dreams
I have this dream
That my True Love and I
Will stand before God
And our families
Publicly Professing
Our love and
Devotion to one another
My children will stand
Beside me
Accepted and Loved
For whom they are
I have this dream
That God will
Grant us a son
Who will be loved
Deeply
By his father
I have this dream
That this son
Will walk the world
Showing God's Love and Peace
And that race is only
An adjective…
Not a verb
I have this dream
That a daughter
Will come with a
Sunshine smile and a
Beautiful heart of Love
I have this dream
God will show the world
Through my poetry
He is alive

Walking the earth
Making Impossible Dreams
Come true
I have this...
Beautiful Dream of
God's mighty presence
And Love for this world
Where Love and
True hearts are
Abound
I have this Dream!

BELIEVE IN WHAT YOU CANNOT SEE

Believe in what you cannot see
For everything is up to me
Believe that you can be
    Happy
The choice is up to me
Believe that everything is coming
Just as I promised it would be
Believe in what you cannot see
For everything is up to me
Believe in the heavens
    Up above
For that is where you are
    Truly loved
Believe in what you cannot see
For everything is up to me
Believe you will meet
Your True Love again
A smile will light his way
Believe he'll wrap his
Arms around you
In an oh, so gentle way
Believe in what you cannot see
For everything is up to me
He is coming
My child…
He is coming!
I know you cannot see
But everything!
Everything is…
Up to me!
Believe!

Beginnings And Endings

Today was quiet, serene
And peaceful
Snow gently falling
The cold crisp air
Refreshed my spirit
Today was a day of
        Beginnings
For I was calm and quiet
God is loving me and guiding me
He restores my spirit
Today was a new beginning
He is revealing the truth
He shows me he is changing
Other's cold hearts
Yesterday was an ending to
Much strife and ridicule
The icy hearts are melting
The stares are warming
The hugs are not
Cold and untrue
Today is the beginning
Of something God has
Begun anew
Yesterday was the ending
Of all of the strife and
        Ridicule
God loves me and
Guides me
He has begun something
        Anew
Today is a beginning
Of something new

Today was quiet
Peaceful and loving
God has a plan
He nurtures and
Guides me
He helps me understand
Life is full of
Beginnings and Endings
But there is always
Something new
Hope is beginning
To fill my heart
For today God has started
          Something new
It was quiet
It was peaceful
There was love all around
For today is a ...
          Beginning...
                    I never knew!

Soon There Is a Church to Be Built

Soon there is a church
        To be built
The occupants
        Are chosen by me
They have a heart
        For God
        Like no other
Soon there is a church
        To be built
Fellowship and community
        Will reside there
Soon there is a church
        To be built
Showing others
        How to walk
        With God
Soon there is a church
        To be built
Growing families
And reaching out
To communities
        Near and far
Soon there is a church
        To be built
God's guiding the
        Plan
Putting people into place
And providing all
        That is needed
Soon there is a church
        To be built
I may call on

You
To step forward and
Lead
Soon there is a church
To be built!

STARK!

Quiet and still
No life here
Black and white
Everything perfect
No flowers
No signs of life
Stark
A dramatic response
To a warm
Heartfelt
Poem
A colorful world
Changed drastically.
Still
Perfect
Frozen in Time
A row of lights added.
I remember a response.
Like this before
Now, everything Is clear.
Black & White
But that will not erase.
The truth
The truth in your heart
Is locked away.
Frozen
Stark!

BOLD

A bold move
A kind gesture
You approached me
I didn't chase you
A bold move
Walking up to me
Demanding I talk to you
After hurting me so
A bold move
Grabbing my hand at work
Reassuring me you love me
A bold move
After the mess exploded
You reached over for a hug
You nodded to your friend
As if to say
"I've got this covered!"
A bold move approaching me
Every day in the parking lot
And then after the destruction
Approaching me
And walking together with me
Into the school
A bold move
Silencing my voice and my life
A bold move
Expecting me to fall for
The same lies
A bold move
Asking me about
My children's well being
Knowing how much you
Hurt us all

A bold move
But God is here
He is in our lives
Protecting and
Guiding us.
I know he has your hand
I know you turned around
A bold move
Now, you walk with him
Where is the warmth?
Where is the love?
Thank you for telling
The truth
God revealed it from above
He showed me a promise long ago
That you were my true love
He helps me journey on
He tells me it is a hard love
A bold move
I forgive you
Thank you
For telling the truth
I am still standing
But they haven't stopped
Their ways
Of manipulation and control
This is in God's hands
Heaven knows
But
I still believe in the
Happy ever after
Because God and his angels
Revealed it from above
I wait on his guidance
For you are my true love.

YOU FOOLED ME!

You came to me
Asking for help
Suddenly you were
Everywhere I turned
I got out of my car
There you were
I sat for lunch with my
Teaching neighbor
There you were
I walked down the hall
There you were saying, "hello"
I dropped my students
Off for gym
The Inquiries began
Questions about people
In my high school
Questions about
My children's schooling
Asking me for advice
About your nephew
Coming to sit near me
During school assemblies
Asking me to buy
Your favorite cookies
When I shop for my family
Volunteering to carry
My book bag
When I broke my arm
Volunteering to play tennis
To help with my recovery
Your sincerity and warmth
In little notes and cards
You placed in my
School mailbox
You Fooled Me!

SURPRISE!

You surprised me
I didn't think
A celebrity like you
Would be interested in me
But
There you were
Following me around
Calling me on my phone
While I picked up my children
Asking me questions
About my life
It surprised me
Each conversation
I kept thinking
How much we got along
Just talking as friends
You surprised me
When you went home to get that
Old tennis racket
To play with me
You surprised me
When you dressed up
For a thank you
Luncheon date
You surprised me
When you told me
You loved me
You surprised me
When you sent that
Text message
Many years later
You surprised me

When you planted the flowers
In front of your home
You surprised me
Where are you now?

TELL ME YOU LOVE ME

Tell me you love me
I won't say a word
Tell me you love me!
With just one word
Tell me you love me!
Take a chance!
Tell me you love me!
With that familiar glance
Tell me you love me!
In your own sweet
Clever way
Tell me you love me!
Tell me today!
Tell me you love me!
That you are true
Tell me you love me!
So, I won't be so blue
Tell me you love me!
Take a stance!
Tell me you love me!
You've got one more chance
Tell me you love me!
Upon your knees
Tell me you love me!
I'm listening, please
Tell me you love me!
Before it's too late
Tell me you love me!
On our first date.
Tell me you love me!
Try it and see!
Tell me you love me!

Don't make me plea!
Tell me you love me
Today…
      If you see…
The love in my heart
Tell me you love me!
And we will never part!

YOU REMIND ME OF

You remind me of
The joy and love
From above
You remind me of
A smile or a hug
You remind me of
The flowers in the spring
You remind me of
The bells that are about to ring
You remind me of
The blossoms
In my garden
Stretching out for the sun
You remind me of
My heart that is waiting
For my love
You remind me of
The beautiful fall leaves
You remind me of
A gentle summer breeze
You remind me of
The happy puppy kisses
You remind me of
The gentle times
I miss them.
You remind me of
A hand stretched out
In care
Letting me know you are there
You remind me of
The hope in my heart
You remind me of

The soft sweet sigh
In the night
You remind me of
The bright sunlight
You remind me of
A heart overflowing
With love
You remind me of
My true love!

DID YOU SEE MY LOVE TODAY?

Did you see my love today?
Sometimes I see him in my dreams
He seems so lonely
Did you see my love today?
How is he?
Did he have anything to say?
Did you see my love today?
Is he kind and compassionate?
Does he ask of me at all?
Did he see me when I was small?
Did you see my love today?
Did he have any kind words to say?
Did he inquire about my family?
Is he searching down deep in his heart
To find the courage to make a brand-new start?
Did you see my love today?
Did he smile in that friendly way?
Did he laugh and joke in his familiar lighthearted way?
Did he inquire about me today?
Did you see my love today?
Is he dreaming of times to come?
Did he play basketball in the hot sun?
Did you see my love today?
What did he say?
Did he tell you about the father above?
Did he share of his goodness and love?
Did you see my true love today?
I wonder how he is so far away.

TODAY I THOUGHT ABOUT YOU

Today I thought about you
I pictured your smile and your hug
How much it reminds me of my fathers hugs
Today I thought about you
In the quiet
Your smile when I told you
I loved you
Today I thought about you
How you couldn't let go
Of our love and our friendship
Many years ago
Today I thought about you
So, I mustered the courage
To be brave and reach out
To see if you still care
Today I thought about you
When I felt despair
I still believe in the promise
God shown from above
How you deeply love me
And your heart is true
That you will come
To see me very soon
I reached out with bravery
To try one more time
To ask you to love me
And share my life again
Today I thought about you
And how time has changed
I hope you believe in what
God is doing in our lives
For today I thought about you

How have you been?
Do you want to talk about things?
Will you let me in?
Today I thought about you
Did you receive my text?
No answer yet!
Silence.
God says, "Wait on him!"

SOMETIMES WHEN IT IS QUIET

Sometimes when it is quiet
I lose hope
That someday I'll see you again
Sometimes when it is quiet
I think about you holding my hand
Helping me to understand
The devastation at hand
Sometimes when it is quiet
I feel your love
You turn to smile
And scratch your head so
Sometimes when it is quiet
I think of your heart
How I could tell when it was warm
And when it was ice cold
Sometimes when it is quiet
I think of your face
How it looked so lovingly
Sometimes when it is quiet
The silence is serene
Because my God is holding onto my heart
Reassuring me
All is not lost
Sometimes when it is quiet
I pray
For God's love and promises
To shine in the light of day
So, I can freely tell you
I love you today.
Sometimes when it is quiet
God is holding my hand.

WAITING ON PRINCE CHARMING

Waiting...Waiting...Waiting...
On Prince Charming
His dark brown eyes
And his contagious
Smile
Are imprinted on
Cinderella's Heart
Waiting...Waiting...Waiting...
On Prince Charming
Cinderella remains steadfast
Dutiful and bright
She sings a cheerful song
Of love and life
And happily, ever after's
Waiting...Waiting...Waiting...
On Prince Charming
Cinderella awaits on
That memorable kiss
And loving look
As blush engulfs his face
Waiting...Waiting...Waiting...
On Prince Charming
Cinderella daydreams
Of him holding
Her hands and
Dancing her first dance
With her True Love
Waiting...Waiting...Waiting...
        On
Prince Charming!

CHAPTER EIGHT

Reconciliation

God has given me peace and calm. I am writing poetry again. I am appreciating all that he has done. But God is always working in our lives. So…this last chapter…Reconciliation.

God wants me to lay down the past. Reconcile and forgive those who believed in the lies and threw the stones. Those who have intentionally hurt me and my family. Those who fooled me! This has been hard. But the more I forgive the better I feel. God wants peace and forgiveness. My load is lighter. He shares with me the future and His promises. He wants me to keep looking for the rainbows and the miracles! Look for the love in life!

"So that man shall say, Verily there is a reward for the righteous: verily he is a God that judgeth in the earth.: Psalms 58:11 KJV

RECONCILIATION

Reconciliation
Forgiving and letting go
Of the past
Reconciling our differences
Forgetting about the pain of the past
Keeping only the sweet memories
Reconciliation
Remembering what is good
The lessons learned
The trials that tested you
Relief that they are over
Reconciliation
Shedding the old ways
Shaping you with tiny lessons
Remembering all that is of God
Forgetting to regurgitate the enemies voices
Reconciliation
Moving forward with a renewed hope
That what is promised will soon come
That there is hope
To spread love and letting go of the bitterness
That you were forced to endure
Reconciliation
Coming closer to God
In the safety of his arms
Surrounded by his Angels
A safe haven of love
Where your life is renewed
New Life is here
Celebrate it!
Reconciliation

SUPPORT CHRISTIAN FAITH

Support Christian Faith
It can be arduous at times
Opinionated people
Following Jesus
Support Christian Faith
Even though righteous people
Hurt you so
Remember Jesus walked these storms
Support Christian Faith
Believe people can change in time
But stay closer to the Father
He knows the way
Support Christian Faith
Tithe when you can
Stand up strong to your adversaries.
Never give up!
Trying times are shaping thee
Support Christian Faith
Look them in the eye
Walk quietly
God knows the truths
Support Christian Faith
It isn't perfect
But we are all here together
Trying to follow Jesus
From the dark
Into the light
Support Christian Faith
Hold onto the good
Remember in the rain
I am here
Believe

God has a purpose in all things
Support Christian Faith
Free your soul of the strife
Let go of the past
It's holding you down
Support Christian Faith
Let your wings take flight
Do what you feel is right
Speak only good
Walk in Faith, Love and Hope
Support Christian Faith
Remember when you were
In the dark
Frightened and alone
Abused and lost
Support Christian Faith
Help tell those searching
For the love that Jesus brings
Understand why we are chosen
To walk this path
In the light and the love
Support Christian Faith

SMALL GROUP

When you are ready my child
When you are ready
You may return to small group
I need you there
My witness
Of my love and devotion to others
When you are ready my child
I know you have been hurt
By others for so long
But I need you to return
To stand strong in my light
When you are ready my child
Great things are at hand
I need you to help shape them
Small Group
Is to support and guide others
During trials and tribulations
The past did not last
For it ran its course
You are loved
You are accepted
I picked you!
You will lead a small group again
Hold on
When you are ready
The discerning eyes will be there
The gossipers will be there
The ones with the stones will still
Be there
But I have taught you to walk stronger
And how to protect your family
Small Group

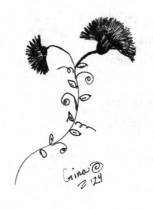

THERE IS A BLESSING

There is a blessing
God bestows on us all
The fierce protection
Of life and love
Cherish your children
Give kindness to all
There is a blessing
God has brought
To tell you
He loves you
And your life
Is worth more than you Thought!

THINK

Think of your family
Think of their love
Think of the value
Of all God's love
You have a treasure
Beyond compare
You have God's love
That you will
Be able to share

I KNOW YOU ARE HERE

I know you are here
I feel you quieting my heart
I see the wonders of
Your work
In the quiet moments
I know you are here
The sun is shining
Inviting me outside before dusk
You walk with me
Settling my worries
And giving me
Peace and calm
I know you are here
Because you settle my fears
Hope is here
You carry me from the
Mountains into the valleys
And you raise me up again
I know you are here
You bring my attention
Into the present
A smile, a hug
Hearts full of love
I know you are here
When now, I see a
Dove
I know this quiet peace
It stills my soul
I am wrapped in your
Eternal love
I have hope!

Gina© '24

TURNING PAGES

God is turning the pages
Of my life
When I have fear
He comforts me and helps
Me to journey on
He turns the page
I have difficulty moving
God is turning pages
Of the story of my life
He helps me reflect upon
What he has carried me through
And why these things happened
God is turning the pages
Of the book of my life
He has a purpose
A beautiful dream
Of my life
He needs me to fulfill
He walks me through
The difficult times
He gives me rest
God is turning the pages
Of my life
So, I may become your wife.

THERE IS A SILENCE

There is a silence
Of Peace and Love
It isn't a silence
Of hurt and pain
There is a silence
That nurtures your soul
And heals your heart
There is a silence
No one can control
The silence of stillness
Love and contentment
There is a silence
Only God knows
Of love and healing
Of just being....
      Quiet....
There is a silence
A calm....
None compares...
To the silence
Of sitting at rest
With your Savior
A love none compares
There is a silence
Your heart is content
Your soul is happy
Worries melt away
There is a silence
The silence of peace
With God
A unity with mankind
A soul searching

Peace
A baby brought to the world
Seek him….
Always!

HOPE

The dream that
Your heart draws
You near
The hope that all
Will be well
In the end
Following a path
You can't see
The destination
But you are
Drawn and inspired
To pursue
Hope
The best of you
Seeking to follow
The journey
Our savior
Sent you on
Hope
To pursue a dream
Written on your heart
That your savior needs
You to fulfill
For the benefit of mankind
Hope
Inspiring others
Along the way
Touching them with
The love the Savior
Taught you
Hope
A chain of

Hearts of gold
Passing on…
The message of His love
And acceptance
The Savior
Wants others
To know….
Hope!

FORGET ME NOT 2

When I am old and gray
I will still have
Something to say
Forget me not!
When my children are grown
I will never be alone
Because their laughter
And tears
And all of their fears
Are in my heart
Forget me not!
When trouble seems imminent
And there seems
Nowhere to turn
Pray to the Father
Read a poem or two
He has given me
Forget me not
When my eyes are
Still shining blue
Throughout all of my
Long years
Forget me not!
When I am quiet
And peace is in
My heart
Hold my hand
Forget me not!
When all I can do
Is look into your
Brown eyes that twinkle
At me

When our hearts lock
And our kisses are
soft and slow
Forget me not!
Remember my dreams!
God gave me
Came true
Remember all the love
On my heart
I poured out to
My family
Forget me not!
Hold my hand
In the quiet
Remember our extraordinary
Journey with Jesus
Is not over
Forget me not
Look into the eyes
Of my children and know
My love is still here
Nothing can keep me
From you
Forget me not!

REMEMBER ME!

Remember me
At the first dawns light
Remember how I found you
Lost in the night
Remember me
When you were scorned
Remember the pain of the
Crown of thorns
Remember me
Each time you lay
Down to sleep
Remember how
The angels sang to you
Remember the comfort
Of your Father's arms
How I kept you
From great harm
Remember the soldier
I taught you to be
Remember how to stand strong
Remember the warnings
The sounds of alarm
Remember when you could not sleep
Remember the shadows
Of deep fear
Remember the crying
And how I dried every tear
Remember the stones
That were thrown
During your grieving
Remember your Father
Protected you from

Their stinging
Remember the cold and vicious
Stares
How lonely it was
When nobody cared
Remember your Father
From up above
Showed you how
You are eternally loved
Remember how to stay
Steadfast and true
Remember each lesson
He taught you
Remember each miracle
You witnessed
Remember His strength
And his tender love
Remember my child....
                    ...your Lord from above!

THERE IS A WONDEROUS STORY

There is a wonderous story
That we are compelled to share
The story of our Father's
Unending love
There is a wonderous story of a great man
He came for the Father
And did all that He planned
There is a wonderous story
Of the love of a
Father and son
Who resides up above
The closeness and bond
Are none to compare
But a Father's love
For His only son
Brought a world of love
Gifted from above!

DO YOU JUDGE PRAYER?

Do you judge prayer?
Who should judge prayer?
No one!
Prayers are from the heart
To the Father
For through Him
All things come
Do you judge prayer?
Who amongst you
Judges the heart
Of another in prayer?
You should be ashamed
Of yourself!
Who are you
To sit on the
Throne of the Father?
All prayer is heard
All prayer is respected
All prayer that is
Faithful
The Father hears
Open hearts pray
To the Father
In love
There is no judgement in prayer
All prayer is useful
In guiding others
To seek His name
Do you judge prayer?
Who are you to tell
Others
Their prayer isn't right?

Only the Father
Sits on the throne
In heaven
Humility, loving kindness,
And peace
Are here in heaven
Do you judge the prayers
Of others?
Not if you have a true heart
For God
Because God so loved
His children that
He listens to their hearts
And prayers
Who should judge prayer?
No one.............!

THE BACKYARD

Sweetly sings the robin
Just outside my window
Early in the morning
He is welcoming a
New day
Whistling a happy tune
Along comes Mr. Squirrel
To release all of the food
From the feeder
He is a crafty guy
Plucking out each beak cover
While hanging upside down
Here comes the love birds
A male and female cardinal
Chasing one another about
The grand trees
In the backyard
Everything becomes quiet
As the sun begins to glow
And sets on the horizon....

SUNLIGHT

Sunlight beams through the trees
The sun is rising
In the early morning breeze
Birds are chirping everywhere
Waking up without a care
Sunlight is glistening
On the pond
Ducks are dipping there
Feet in the water
Geese are stretching their
Long necks
Waddling behind them
Their little ones
Sunlight is rising
Above the clouds
Shinning softly
Across the blue skies
Whipper Whirl !
Hooty Hoot!
Owls are sleeping
The robins are getting
Their young some food
Nestled up high
In the tall trees
Squirrels are scurrying around
Searching for food to store
For the very young
Sunlight is fading
The day is done
Casting bright colors
Across the sky
The moon is rising

In the distance
Casting glowing beams
Into the night
Goodnight....... Sunlight!

GOODNIGHT

Goodnight to my family
Goodnight to my love
Goodnight to the Father
Up above
Goodnight to my children
God bless them
And dry all of their tears
Goodnight to my puppy
God sent with his love
Goodnight to the Angels
Who sing to me
From above
Goodnight to my sweetheart.
It has been many years
God loved us and
Guided us
All of these years
Goodnight to the sunset
Goodnight to the stars
Goodnight to the moon
That glows up above
Goodnight
I Love You!
I whisper off to sleep
God sends me his promises
In my sweet dreams
Goodnight, Goodnight
God wraps me in His love
My daddy sends his
Warm everlasting hugs

Goodnight, Goodnight
As I drift off to sleep my sweetheart's father
Touches my cheek
Goodnight.......

THERE IS A STORM

There is a wind that blows
Across the sea
Strong and steady
But no one really sees
There is a storm
Brewing far away
Late at night
We bow and pray
For safety and perseverance
We sail on our way
There is a Prescence
That settles our souls
And gives us courage
There is a mighty power
Deep in our hearts
He steadies our voyage
And dissolves our fears
When the storm is upon
The sea
He comes to give courage
To help us navigate
He is there
Guiding the way
He calms the fierce waves
And throws out a
Ball of light
Glimmers of colors
Far off in the sunlight
Promises…. Promises….
                    Never to forsake us!
Giving us hope
And the strength to

Journey home
At the gates of heaven
Where we will find
We've always known......

GOD DOESN'T WANT US TO STAY

God doesn't want us to stay
When someone is hurting us
God loves us
He protects us
He guides and nurtures us
We are not meant to endure
Pain from someone else's
Infliction
This is not love
This violence
Breaks any covenant
Seen by God
God is love
Pain inflicted by another
In the perception of
Love
Is not Love
Therefore
It is not of God
God doesn't want us to stay
And endure violence
In any form
He wants us to love,
Grow, learn and extend
Kindness to others
He wants us to be generous
God loves us
He knows our hearts
God doesn't want us to stay
When others are inflicting pain
Upon us
We are strong in Him

He is our fortress
Our armor and shield
God wants us to be free
To love and be loved
God doesn't want us to stay!

LOOKING FOR THE MIRACLES

God has given me peace in my life. He shelters and guides me each day. It took me awhile to release all my fears. God has taught me to let them go and trust in Him. Many times, throughout my journey with Him he has shown my fears to be false. Now, he lifts me up. He shows me the beauty that surrounds me. He encourages me to look for the miracles that God brings.

If you would have told me two years ago, I would be living in my own home again, I wouldn't have believed it. Now, today I am sitting by my pool on a beautiful sunny day listening to the water trickle and enjoying this silence. This truly is a miracle!

Gina

WATCHING FOR A MIRACLE

I stand and watch for
        A miracle
        A miracle
I stand and watch for
        A miracle
        A miracle
Grace has found me
God is around me
He is bringing
        A miracle
Standing silent
        Hope and love
        Surrounds me
God is calming
        My every fear
He has dries off
        Every tear
I stand and watch for
        A miracle
        A miracle
Hope has found me
Love surrounds me
I wait in silence
        For a miracle
Some will see me
In this big place
They don't remember
How I ran this race
But, God picked me up
I saw His face
Hope surrounds me
Love has found me
Now I wait…
        For a miracle
God is bringing a… Miracle!

LOVE IN LIFE

In the morning
Just before dawn
Listen for my guidance
To press on
Listen carefully
To your Father above
He wants to grant you
So much love
When you are weary
Frustrations are strong
Let go
You don't have to hang on
Anymore
I am here
To bear these burdens
I will clear the way
Listen for the direction
I am giving
I am helping you
        On your way
To the life I have promised
It isn't too good to be true
It is a promise of love
And it is just for you
Sent from above
In the morning
Wake up with a smile
Great things are happening
You will run and dance
You have a chance
At true love
Remember to thank the Father

Up above
The strife is over
Love life and enjoy
The simple beauty that
Cannot be bought
All will be provided
So, fear not
Remember the lessons
Remember the comforts
From the angels above
Remember...
                    The Love in Life!

Printed in the United States
by Baker & Taylor Publisher Services